I
Will
Adore
You

I Will Adore You

© 2021 Charna Ainsworth

August Publishing

ISBN: 978-1-7351149-1-0

I Will Adore You *is dedicated to Christ Fellowship Church in Dawsonville, Georgia.*

A special thank you to Phillips, Craig & Dean for Revelation Song.

Without the love and support of my family and friends I would not have pursued my passion for writing. Thank you so much, Dad, Mom, Greg, Maria, Haley, Paige, and Paulyn.

Table of Contents

Chapters of Grace

Upon waking
I feel You here with me.
The sun fills sleepy eyes
thankfulness leaves my lips
before my feet touch the floor.
How I ever lived
without You,
only the thief would understand.
Oh, the years that were stolen
the days Your plans
for my life
stood still…
the page unturned,
chapters of grace
simply erased by evil…
pursuing me with broken promises
never fulfilled,
because of Your love for me.

Heart Made of Gold

See within my mind's eye
do it if you dare.
Look beyond the outer walls
poisoned by judgment,
tattered by disrepair.
Would you find me pretty,
if you found a heart made of gold?
When you looked upon the part…
with His name etched so deep,
learned of His wondrous thoughts
solely towards me,
meant only to edify and strengthen you.
Life is built
one day at a time.
A firm foundation
is a solution
to the universal
        -wasted time.
You can see what you want to see,

take whatever in order to find

    …your way.

I'm only a brick, maybe two

used to pave this path called life.

I Will Adore You

My life is not my own
I laid it down willingly
to become a reflection
of the one my eyes
have yet to see.
He met me in the shadows...
whispered my name...
gathered me out of darkness
where I could be reborn.
He reminded me I'm a child
and would never be left alone.
I'm undone
in the presence of Him now,
unaffected by man
or what he could do.
My path is chosen...
all my days
I will adore You.

charna ainsworth

Man Made Light

Wrapped inside your arms so tight
no beginning, no end within the light
whispers of truth, direction and plans
of days apart in a foreign land
ears that barely hear
what this heart perceives
of duty and mission
bound upon a soul
that is eternal, everlasting…
void of the present truth
of the lives most lead,
full of hatred and greed,
rebounding from pain to inflict pain.

Oh, that I had never come this way.

Maybe......... He asked,

believing I could be one strong enough

to complete this task

of loving

with very little reason to love,

of forgiving

when forgiveness is far from easy,

of sharing…

the truth about heaven.

This body entraps my spirit

but holds no control

      over my soul.

It shines brighter

than any man-made light

you have ever seen.

One day you will know

and you will be known.

He will be there to greet you

if you make it home,

He'll ask, "Did you learn to love?"

The answer will already be known.

My Vessel

You see me like no one else could.
They look at my face,
judge me by my body,
like or dislike my clothes.
Their eyes send messages
and within seconds
I have been placed
on the like or dislike list,
but You see past
my outer shell
straight to the heart
of everything
that's truly me
yet You still love
all that I am,
all that I will be
today, tomorrow
and for all eternity.

Forgive Myself

I found You at the end of my rope
silently standing,
not a mean word to say
about the foolish games
in this life I had played...
I was so naive
always looking to the past
never fully understanding
how You could forget and forgive
all the things I've done wrong,
or how Your love could heal...
how someday I would be strong.
I would forgive myself
because You want me to
and begin a new life
that is only found in You.

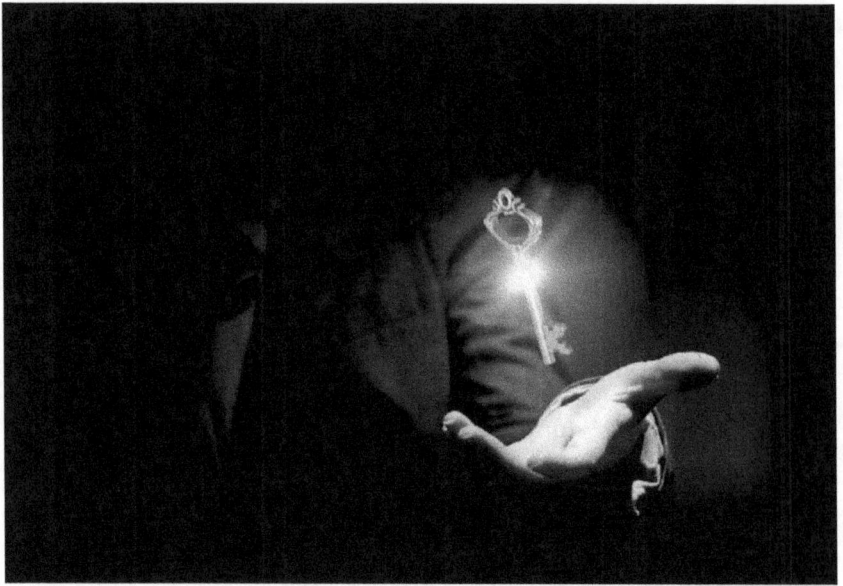

A Thousand Walls

Leading ever so gently...

Your voice

heard by the heart.

You judged...

unequivocally found worthy

because of your name

etched in red

from scriptures memorized

while speaking aloud

valiantly declaring victory

over the stronghold

their narrow judgment

placed upon my life.

The key in hand

to unlock one thousand doors

to crumble a thousand walls

     unable to contain

     -love.

But tell me...

Who could contain Him?

Certainly not me,

anymore.

Written in Red

When I feel that no one's there
and I'm so alone,
hands that hurt
words that stab
lies upon his lips…
beaten and bruised,
I gave my heart to You
on faith and a prayer
that his hands
would no longer touch me
and Your words
     written in red
could heal my wounds
then truth and life
should be forever
on my lips
rewriting a life story
to more closely resemble His.

Still Small Voice

One day it will be too late
for you to change your mind
and your fate
of eternal separation from the One
who loved you so,
gave His life just to show
how much you really mean.
The silent whisper began
when you were just a kid
but you pushed Him away
like an imaginary friend.
The voice spoke louder
when rebellion came calling
before you were eighteen
but you refused to listen
and certainly not to Him.
This voice became calmer
as you approach thirty
but you were too busy

to even listen

or take time to think about Him.

Then the voice was rarely heard

as the burdens of life

weighed upon your soul

but instead of listening

your only thought was He's to blame.

Now no voice remains

except for your own

escaping from lips

that speak of what your eyes see.

Darkness, darker than it's even possible…

no light will you ever see

for all eternity.

My Beautiful Name

The liar and thief came knocking on my door.
Without hesitation the knob twisted in my hand.
Pulling blindly, I let the darkness in…
no more than a young girl.
Without parental supervision
or guiding love to shield…
you would say I was a victim
but there was nothing left to steal.
My vessel was empty;
until I became quiet,
hidden in the dark
and I heard Him gently
call out my name.
One beam of light fell,
then the darkness went away
and the look on your face…
such pity
such distaste
faded away…

within my memory banks

replaced by the *One*

who whispered my name.

My Neighbor

You with your prying eyes,
judgment falling
from lying lips...
tell me...
did I ever ask
for any of this?
Reverse the years
of when you could have been,
should have been kind...
but without your hate
I'm not sure
Jesus would have become
a friend of mine.
So no regrets
no unforgiveness
tying me down to what could have been.
The times I stayed quiet
and didn't make a sound

I've given it all to the Holy One
who'll never abandon me.

Yes, unlike you...

Jesus will always be there.

Anointed

Wasted years
loving the wrong man
watching the time slip away
like sand falling
through my hands.
I worshiped the flesh
made by Your hands
instead of worshipping You,
the One who holds me
in the palm of His hand.
Foolish child,
desperate for love…
seeking and searching,
never stopping or thinking
You were enough.
What sadness to look back…
on a life so incomplete
until the day
You filled me with Your love
and with holy oil anointed me.

This Life Speaks

Looking across a star filled sky
drinking deep this moment in time
feeling drawn to invisible light
surely coming from gentle eyes.
Watching Your dearly beloved
though her eyes do not see;
A desperate heart beats slowly
to the whisper of her name.
This life speaks of problems
all requiring a fix,
fleshly body deceives a pure spirit
that speaks a love language
created before the world began.
They teeter between
Your heart and mine…
intercede, I plead;
Show me Your glory.

I Will Adore You

24

Harder to See

You saw my innocence slip away
in a moment
of becoming a demented man's prey,
threats rolling off the tongue
toward the young and precious one
You called years before
in a moment
of becoming a savior's daughter.
Crashing through the loneliness,
shattering all the words
spoken over me.
How did it feel, Father?
To watch what was happening to me…
to witness the divide of my soul.
Each time,
with every crime,
made it harder to see…
…You.

Homecoming

Fields of flowers all in bloom
radiant sunshine streaming through

clouds of white in a blue sky
You in the midst... arms stretched out wide.
Running... impassioned,
Love at first sight.
Drawn into the light coming from your eyes.
Our embrace must wait as I fall to my knees
ashamed of the times
I thought You forgot about me.
Face first into lush green grass...
silent tears falling

then I hear You say…

well done, my child

now you're home to stay.

The Old Me

Who am I without You?

An empty vessel.

No destination in sight.

A lost child without a home.

A brightly colored kite,

with no string to hold it.

I'm nothing… if I don't have You.

Now when I remember

how shallow my thoughts use to be,

the way no one else mattered,

it was all about me

until Your blood covered my sins

and Your love rescued me.

A Plan and Purpose

It's not for you to understand
the path that you've been led to walk
only to walk and believe.
What's best... where you're walking to
or what you're walking through
is not always a test,
remember?
I've got plans for you,
A purpose for your life…
if you listen quietly
my voice will be your guiding light
through troubles, happiness, and pain;
I've experienced them all
in order to gain
your love and devotion
in a world falling apart…
when you are not of the world
My love will fill your heart,
your peace will surpass all understanding

as you kneel to pray,

I'll open the door for you;

just know, we will be together

now and for always.

He Loves Me

Rescued from all troubles.
Counted among the redeemed.
Brought up from the pit
of mankind's dirty deeds.
Washed with the blood
that testifies the Son of man
is one with the living God.

Who is able to forget,
who is able to forgive
everything wrong I ever did
to every person I've ever known
including the one
He loves so dearly
-Me.

There is only one…

What He Said

To be loved like that

to be cherished and understood.

To be important,

to be cared for...

to just feel good.

To be protected,

to be sheltered beneath His wing...

to know He meant every word He said about me.

I am free.

I am sanctified.

I am victorious.

I am redeemed.

Free... John 8:36

Sanctified... 1st Corinthians 6:11

Victorious... 1st John 5:4

Redeemed... Ephesians 1:7

Overflowing Heart

My eyes will not look to the north or the east;

they are fixed toward the hills.

When I'm in need I'll call out Your name,

to my aid You will come.

By Your design, by Your plan, I need only whisper...

The answer is heard.

I know Your voice Lord, I know Your voice!

Now I understand why the veil is thin

and this longing for You never ceases to end.

To think of Your love for me... tears begin to flow.

When I look back on my days, I see so much wasted time,

but it's not what You see because You know my heart
is overflowing with the spirit You graciously gave to me.

Building Their House

What do you teach your children
when no one else can see
      no one can hear?
Is it love and compassion
or is it hate and fear?
You think you're safe
behind those closed doors
but little eyes see
little ears hear
and remember forevermore.
If you taught love and compassion
blessed will be your name
rolling off the tongue
of your children's children.
If you taught hate and fear
even the first generation
will turn their back and run
and you will reap eternally
for the love you didn't give

and the regret of what

your compassion could have done.

Home Sweet Heaven

Never in my wildest dreams
could I have imagined love like this…
overflowing,
uncontainable,
His mercy - His favor
no more striving
no more worry
I've been completely set free
the prison doors are open
angels are singing,
I've become everything
He wanted me to be.
Full of light,
full of spirit,
full of His love
pouring over,
pouring out,
His glory surrounds me.
I speak His language… He listens,

praises fill the air,

the anointing lingers

I'm lost in forever and ever

but I know I'll find Jesus there.

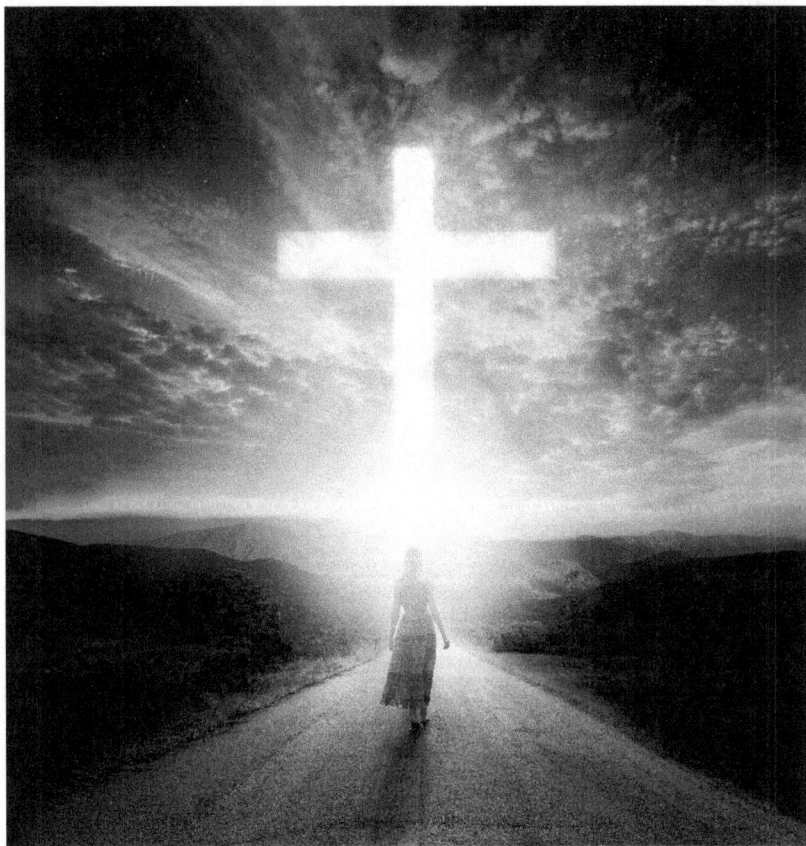

Two Words

Jesus wept.

Saint John

Chapter 11

Verse 35

The shortest, most powerful verse written

about love in the New Testament.

It's the period that always gets me.

Two words; one huge 'period'

which stops the reader

allowing the heart

to feel

to know

their savior was really a man

with feelings similar to every person ever born

on this alien planet called earth.

The tears that fell

from His caring eyes

saw the world

like none of us do

because His compassion

for us…
never fails
it never ends.
He would walk to the ends of the earth
to find the lost,
the ones given to Him.
When He wept because Mary fell at His feet
Jesus wept because His spirit was deeply moved,
not with hatred
not with spite
but with the purest love for those who die
without His name written on their hearts
and for the ones who are too badly hurt
to know the truth
standing right before their eyes.
When He's accepted
no one ever truly dies
they're only asleep
as they close their eyes
shake off their bodies
slip past the veil
where they are fully alive
in the holy one,
the one who wept
and brought Lazarus back to life.

Give You My Heart

Closer and closer
my true love draws closer to me
it's because Jesus can plainly see
the condition of my heart
after your hate fueled rage...
the words you spewed
like shards of glass ripping it apart
with each syllable
every ugly word
breaking
what I've given to You.
Broken...
I fall to my knees
crying out for justice
crying out for peace
drawing a circle of light
to surround You and me
giving You
what already belongs

no longer a gift

no longer a mystery

just another broken heart.

charna ainsworth

45

He Knows

How do I stand in this world of make believe?
Falsehood and fakery,
illusions and scams…
almost every human trying to grab
what's theirs and what isn't.
There I am with hope and trust,
blindly believing in someone
most of the world
could never see…
is the only way,
the only One for me.
He holds eternity
in His hand.
He whispers my name
He knows the plan
He wrote it down
so long ago…
it's in a book in heaven
with a name as the title

a name He knows…

Charna.

One Drop of Blood

Trusting in the unseen

never followed… nor heard one word aloud

spoken by the man

wanted; within a crowd of liars, of sinners, and thieves.

Innocent……. they drew blood.

Innocent……. they laughed and mocked.

Innocent……. they drove the nails

piercing… the savior of the world.

One drop… I'm set free.

One drop… and you can be free.

No bondage can hold what truly belongs surrendered at the cross…

just let it go…

nothing is too much, no burden too heavy

His life for your life;

nothing less than abundant.

Omnipresent

You are here
You are there
You are everywhere I go
You are near to me
every step of the way
giving me strength day after day.
I search and I find Your sweet precious love
one of a kind, sent down from heaven above
to guide me, to lead me
down the long and winding path, we call life
without You I would be blind
stumbling, falling
no light I would see
there would be no one to rescue me
from darkness
from sadness
from despair
So- as I rise;
I seek You every day...
You are here.

You and Me

Golden yellow sunlight reaches down past the clouds
bathing every single thing the eye can see
like gentle waves of love swelling in an endless sea
only known by you and me…
The last beautiful souls around who dare to dream
never giving up, never backing down
regardless of how it looks
or how far we must reach.
Always full of belief when others would have folded…
our hands are filled with cards.
The dealer is a monster.
The dealer rules this world.
He knows only the strong survive
after he throws everything at them,
     at their lives.
The few come through the fire,
the few come out as gold.
These are the ones who didn't sell their souls.
They gave them freely to the One who knows…

the One who wrote books about their lives
before they were ever born
and the dreams were placed in hearts
within their mother's womb.
Dreams to take them places
dreams that lead to home…
tho the way be troublesome
tho the way be long.
The One placed a burning desire
into these two hearts.
The passion for success
never wavers
never passes,
it's always at the surface
just below everything we do,
believing when the time is right
all our hopes and dreams will come true.

Chasing After You

Into the depths...
dive deeply
never rising
completely consumed within Your eyes,
transfixed by Your words.
Never going back.
Never going to quit...
chasing after You with all I have.
Pedal to the metal,
no destination too far
all I really know is I must be
wherever You are.
High on a mountain,
low in the valley
beside a gentle stream
in a field of daffodils;
No matter the location
my place is with You...
I'd follow to the ends of the earth,

anywhere I'll go

just as long as we're together

because there's no way

I'm living this life without You.

I Am Yours

You follow me
through the wilderness
into the sea
can't imagine
there's any place
You wouldn't come
to be with me.
It was nothing I said,
nothing I did,
no hoop did I jump thru...
still, you love me
like no one else ever could
because I am Yours.
Not a moment of time
morning, noon, or night
that Your angels don't watch over me.
Your Holy Spirit resides
inside my heart...
Your gentle voice guides me.

So it's You that I follow…

like a sheep follows a shepherd.

When this life is over, I'm coming home.

There… You and I will be together forever.

Front Porch View

Cool breeze upon my skin

Blue skies as far as the eye can see

Green grass popping up through brown leaves

First flowers of the year

Open their petals to bloom

Songbird gently sings

Cat meows, sitting next to me

Out on the horizon

A storm cloud begins to loom

As puppy awakes to play.

These are the happenings

of a beautiful spring day.

Out in the country…

from the view

of my front porch.

It's a Mississippi March morning,

something to be grateful for…

soon the spring will turn to summer

and the heat will come in waves,

then I will miss these cool spring mornings

remembering them fondly

within the memories of this day.

Because I Follow

You were not afraid

to stand before the crowd

speaking the truth

whether Your message was loved or hated,

followed by those who loved You

chased by those who hated.

You always escaped; until surrender.

I'll always escape because of You.

There'll be a door, a window, an open gate

for me to walk through.

I'll never be alone because I follow You.

A small still voice, I hear in my heart

tells me not to fear

whispers light in the dark

of courage and strength, I didn't know I had

to stand in front of the crowd

and be proud that I did.

Write the words, prepare the speech,

set the scene of all the dreams I've been given.

This is the most daunting…

the hardest to begin

because I don't like what I see when I watch me.

The scars

INVISIBLE

…but I see.

The confidence

UNSHAKEABLE

…crumbles within.

There's only one way,

one way indeed,

So I call out to You…

You give me strength

to turn on the camera

to speak into the mic…

looking in your eyes

makes everything alright.

I can open up, I'm vulnerable now

they can hate me

they can love me

but the fear is gone; it's all over now.

I can fulfill my calling without guilt and shame.

You give me the strength,

You called me by name.

I ANSWERED.

Favorite Psalm

I don't want to be ashamed
because I put my trust in You.
Show me Your ways, my Lord
I don't want to be afraid,
teach me Your paths
I don't want to be lost,
not even for a day.
Guide me in Your truth
I don't want to go astray,
You are my God
the only hope I have
is found in You.
I don't want to be ashamed
when You remember my youth
all the mistakes I've made
when I didn't know
Your mercy is greater
than any sin I knew.
Remember me, oh Lord

instruct me in Your ways

to be humble and teachable

from this moment until my dying day.

Forgive my iniquity

forgive my wounded heart…

fear overwhelms me now;

my eyes may drift from gazing upon You,

when they do have mercy and remember I am lonely and afflicted…

my enemies hate me more and more it seems.

Will You come and rescue me?

Please, don't let me be ashamed… because You, oh Lord…

You are my everything.

Like a Shadow

It took so long
but looking back
I see You were there
more than I knew
more than I could see…
standing so close
not close enough to see
watching over
never abandoning
never leaving
or saying goodbye.
In the moment
peace was elusive
almost unknown…
I was the shepherd's daughter
in the enemy's world.
No compassion,
nor church to grow up in…
only hatred

only sin.

Without Your love

there's no telling

where I would be...

certainly not here

probably not at peace,

sitting calmly

as my enemies flee

with You still beside me.

Oh! Your Presence

When you see me again
you will not see my face
even though we'll be friends.
My spirit will ignite the holy ground
where you stand.

In Your glory, my lips will touch the streets of gold.
As You whisper my name…
I believe You will say, 'Well done, my child.'

I imagine tears streaming down my face
Your presence...
Oh! Your presence
is all I long for.

Lifting my head to look towards You
is so much more than I deserve.
Still, here I am…
I ran the race, now I'm finally home.
Just to be near You is more than enough

eyes shut tighter,

worshipping You while You're near

I feel Your presence coming closer still.

The angels, their voices moving toward me

I feel a hand touch my back.

A voice inside says arise… come, go with Me.

There's no hesitation, nothing to resist… I go.

I follow You to a grand banquet

to a celebration, like none that's ever been before

and the likes will never be again.

I sit not far from my king…

He kisses my cheek,

He calls me friend.

He says the fight is over.

He won!

Now… eternity can begin.

Birthdays

Nobody knows the way this feels
to them it's just another day.
The spring flowers are in bloom,
the sunshine falls in rays,
yet no amount of searching
will reveal your handsome face.
Not even if I cried
or called out your name.
No, nothing will bring you near.
There's not one thing that can be done,
nothing to undo…
to change fate
or what happened to you
on your final day.

Remembered

What do we do on the days
when we would be celebrating
the birth of our loved ones who passed away?
They are no longer here to blow out the candles
to make a wish…
there are no photographs to take,
no presents to open or memories to create.
Still, it's their birthday,
it's impossible to ignore or not
remember how old they would have been.
What do you do when you're not sure?
What's deemed appropriate for our departed loved ones?
Maybe it's best to remember them,
just as you would want to be remembered.
It's within our hearts and minds
that we keep the memory of our loved ones alive.
Special to us are certain days,
when we remember their lives
and the special love they gave.

Tell Him Jesus

Jesus, when You see him in heaven
will You tell him I said hello?
It feels like forever since I've seen his face
and I guess he's wondering if I'm doing okay,
so if you happen to talk
please let him know
I think about him from time to time,
wondering why he had to pass away before me...
and how long will it be before I see him again.
Please Jesus, tell him not to worry...
... now I remember that doesn't happen there.
If he asks again, how I'm doing... don't answer him.
Avoid the subject;
just start talking about Your promises that You fulfilled
after being nailed to the cross,
that we will see each other again
when my race is won
and we can never really be totally apart
in heaven or on earth

because I've still got a part of him

right here in my heart.

Every Word

The gift was given at first breath.

Why did you cry?

Life is precious from beginning to end through the good and bad,

whether happy or sad…

every moment given to learn; to love, is only a moment.

Moments add up, someday...

you'll account for every word that's come out of your mouth.

No wonder wisdom brings great silence…

quiet retrospect of the past and present.

Forgiveness shouldn't be denied, even to our self.

We are in fact …only human,

the gift giver's favorite pet

if we freely give our life to Him.

Sit Down Beside Me

The sun is rising…
its light upon my back.
Cool crisp morning,
dew drops are falling
onto green, green grass.
Birds are singing
happy songs of spring…
I'm gently rocking
on the ole' porch swing.
Distant cars on the highway
say somebody is going somewhere,
American flag waves slowly,
moved by early April air…
dogs are not barking,
perhaps enjoying silence, too.
It's more than beautiful.
What's a poet to do…
but invite you in; Come on into my world,
everything is so green,

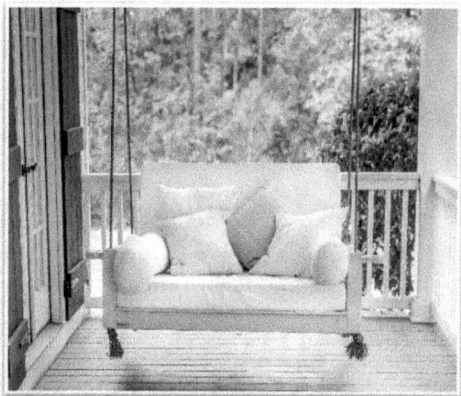

flowers of every color can be seen.

So come... sit down beside me

on this ole' porch swing,

we'll enjoy the silence together.

Quarantine Wishes

Talk to me of better times
yet to come…
moments when I'm with good friends.
When love and laughter are being sown
and weaved into the very thread
of me and them,
where memories spark
with brilliant light
of all that is good
      all that is right
and I'll believe…
I'll hang on
till another day
seeking
searching
finding a way to press back
the sadness
the darkness I've found
by remembering

what it's like to love and to laugh
with good friends around.

Without Regret

Salty water lapping at the edge of the bay,

seasoned voices drift slowly my way

as I approach old lounge chairs.

Out toward the horizon

there's a story being told

so many lives, so many souls

who look across this body of water.

Oh, the tales they tell

of love and loss…

       happiness and pain.

Lifetimes of memories dancing round in their heads,

if I had the key to open the doors;

and thoughts… like waves crash upon the shore.

Would everyone here run toward

or would they run away?

Contemplating it now

it's hard to say…

most people want to know about a person's life,

the mistakes, the triumphs, missed opportunities and success,

while few want their lives displayed for retrospect.

It seems there's one thing that most humans forget-

when you get right down to it, we're all flesh and bones.

So let wisdom speak loudly... never live in fear or regret.

Where Are You God?

The world is crashing down on me
I can't feel You anywhere...
my prayers are not ceasing
in fact, they're increasing
during the turmoil bestowed
upon my life,
mostly made of strife.
Where are You?
Right now, I need You most;
my heart, once so full of love
is crumbling under the weight
of everything I hate
about the world and mankind.
I need You now
but You can't be found.
Where are You?
Have You forgotten me?
I gave my life to You!
Completely surrendered my soul

begging for nothing except You...

leaving my former life behind.

Where are You, God?

If you have forsaken me,

if You have left me

to face this battle alone

then all hope is gone.

Where are You, Jesus?

When I really need a friend?

The ones I had left

when my new life began.

At first it didn't matter,

because no one loves me like You

but now I'm so alone

and I can't find You.

Where are you, Jesus?

Apart From The World

What now, Jesus?

Where do I go?

What do I do?

You know what lies ahead…

I don't want to drift, unless it's drifting to You.

The world is changing… my voice is so small

there are roadblocks everywhere but still,

I want to go…

to be your hands and feet is all I ever wanted,

to love with all my heart

unafraid of what people say.

Set me apart from the world.

I will not play their game…

of chasing after riches that lead to nowhere -

puffing up with foolish pride,

believing that 'things' can change my life for good

when there is nothing good

about envy, lust, and greed.

My life was a gift; I refuse to make it a lie

by wanting and needing everything

except the One who will make it complete.

I'd rather die a martyr's death

then perish without my savior's breath within me.

All Roads Point to You

There's fire in your eyes.

This fire speaks… it says I'm never alone.

It says don't be afraid of what man can do.

Let me help you… have the abundant life.

There is a way that seems right

… but it's wrong.

The Guide can help.

You must be strong.

Invisible War

Everything happens for a reason
but what if that reason
is to kill, steal and destroy?
Seems like this new saying
points the blame to where it doesn't belong,
thinking God would allow
so much drama,
so much trauma
is completely wrong.
There's an invisible war
the naked eye can't see,
it's for your soul
and my soul
to decide where
our eternity will be.
Endure to the end,
run your own race...
words to remember
the next time

a friend or foe says…

'Everything happens for a reason'

trying to make it more acceptable

for the enemy to spit in your face.

We Will Dance

One thousand cords

tie me to you

an instrument of salvation

directing decisions

of outcomes

profound

in a world

a new world

yet to come

not far away

where I will be known

not hidden behind the veil

of queens and daughters,

kings and sons

eternal life will begin,

have no end…

we will dance

we will not cry

we will learn

we will not die

no death or decay

no violence or hate

only love.

Love is My name…

once inside the gates

home is where you'll stay

no more doubts

no more fears

no death, no disease

only love lives here.

In Me

You are in Me

I am in you,

one blood - one body

there's nothing left for you to do.

You don't have to work...

you don't have to strive,

I paid all the cost so you can live abundantly,

be fully alive,

love...

love until giving opens the door.

No judgment.

No hatred, no keeping score...

of what's right, what's wrong

within yourself, or others.

'Abundant life'

does not include

coveting your neighbor

hating your brother

or slandering your mother.

It's about freedom.

You're no longer a captive of sin,

you've been washed clean.

Now go… and live like it.

Not for One Moment

Let me remind you who I am
as you search for meaning and purpose…
when all along, as you're searching
I've written it down in your book;

Written before you were given a name,
full of triumphs, not much pain
commissioned to love, never to hate
provided for from beginning to end

written that someday you would become
My best friend
sheltered under the strength of My promises
protected from being a target
of fallen angels with broken wings.
Yes, before you spoke your first words
all of heaven rejoiced...
they sang, she'll grow up strong,
one day she'll make the choice
of whom to serve... body, spirit, and soul,
then the blessing she'll receive
will be placed in her hands
as she begins to become one
with the Son of Man.
Not for a moment
will I leave her alone.
I'll send to her another
who will whisper... don't be afraid.
I'm the Holy Ghost, the promised one
I'll lead you,
be with you for life
commanding the heavenly angels to move
as He's reading your story
day by day in the glory light

the story that was written

before you drew your first breath

in a world that almost believes

the resurrected Prince of Peace is deceased.

These are the ones who

once faced the same choice-

draw close to their Lord and Savior

or ignore that small still voice…

…just force a stiff upper lip

and go it alone…

never fully understanding

this world is not their home.

So sad they keep searching

for a love they'll never find

most certainly becoming bitter over time;

empty and bankrupt beyond measure

their books lie unopened and dusty

in the Kingdom of heaven

where hearts break no more.

All are welcome…

you need only to answer The Door.

What Good Fathers Do

We belong in the shadow of His love
where everything good is His.
There is darkness in this world...
but none of it is found in Him.
Jesus spoke of our troubles
knowing they would certainly come.
He gave us courage to face every one.
It is written; Do not fear!
Whenever you feel completely alone
I will come to you
I will be near
to comfort, to guide
because that's what good Fathers do.
As you live the days of your life
there's only one thing I ask of you...
choose love.
Choose me...
let My spirit set yours free...
to live in this world
to truly live in peace and harmony.

charna ainsworth

Before Eve Fell

Everyone is searching
hoping to find
a little peace
some measure of happiness
a reason to live
another day
another hour.
Everybody is looking for
their hearts desire…
and the days
when everything seems
to go right,
when it all falls
into place
like the moments
were predestined
before Eve fell from grace…
only to watch it fall apart
like a wrong turn

on an endless path.

Asking why?

What did I do wrong?

Understanding the answers will remain unknown.

Full Possession

It's You, standing in the distance
fire coming from Your eyes
I'm frozen... unable to speak
Like a child, surprised by what they've seen.
Closing my eyes for a moment,
Looking again just to be certain
I've seen what I'm seeing
Do I run to You... fall at Your feet,
worship the One I love...
promise to never leave?
Do I kneel where I'm standing
wait for You to come to me...
praying every moment
You will recognize me.
Your presence is too strong
I'm crushed beneath the weight
face down on the ground
Holy fire begins to penetrate
Every little speck of me that doesn't look like You.

I've never been more happy.

My prayers finally answered.

Take every part of me

until I'm fully possessed by You.

God is in Control

If God was in control
of everything that happened on earth
never would I place my soul in His hands.
Knowing the creator of everything
could allow such tragedy
would be too hard for me to understand.
I'd turn my back and run
faster than an eagle can fly
in the other direction
as far as I could get
away from Christianity.
My mind would ask questions...
the answers plain to see,
if God is in control
where was He...
when I was being raped
when I was being robbed
the moment my child died
while lying in my arms,

the time my boyfriend kicked me

as I was lying on the floor

and in the hallway of high school

surrounded by the mean boys?

If God is in control

why is there so much war?

Every time I hear the news

I have to turn it off

knowing I just can't take anymore.

The God I know

would never dish out disease

to an infant, a mother

or a young boy in need.

Then there's poverty and lack…

if God is in control

would He really allow

His creation to live like that?

These words I'm writing

will probably step on a lot of toes…

someone had to say it,

the world needs to know.

Satan, the devil

Put this line

on the tip of your tongue

making him appear innocent

for all he has done

Killing and raping

stripping dignity from anyone he possibly can,

you see, he is running short of time

in an unwinnable war.

So he runs to and fro...

spreading rumors and lies

destroying every life

one evil act at a time,

... but what an alibi

this wicked Prince has

the whole world bought

one lie rolling off his forked tongue

'God is in control'

Feels so right to deceive everyone.

Every Step of the Way

The good people get up on Sunday morning
get themselves dressed and go to church.
Wish I could be like that...
'Good'
spend an hour and a half
trying to keep my mind from straying
off the words preacher is saying
so I can have a blessed week.
Instead, I'm one of those people
whose love for God can't be contained
by four brick walls on Sunday morning.

My church is here.

My church is there.

My church is everywhere I take a breath.

He's here with me... every step of the way,

when I sleep,

when I eat,

I'm always praying... for more...

more of Him... as much as I can have.

I'm taking 'church' with me...

Monday through Sunday.

His holy fire burning for all the good people

who criticize and despise somebody like me.

The Seed of Desire

Use your imagination,
do it if you dare…
see yourself having the things you want
going places you've never seen
giving away what you want to give.
Is anything impossible to the person who believes?
Speak it out…
give life to your dreams,
watch them unfold as day builds upon day
until that blessed moment when you can finally say…
I wanted!

The seed of desire planted in my heart
I watched
I waited
knowing in time everything I believed
would grow… producing fruit for many to eat
because I am a tree planted near the water's edge
never thirsty,

never alone...

always dreaming

of making this a better world.

I'm Down on My Knees

Oh Lord - let Your glory fall on me
I'm weary and tired
I need Your strength.
Sweet Jesus,
please don't forget about me
I'm a Sinner in need of Your grace
to wash me clean.
My friend,
I'm crying out... don't pass me by,
give me Your mercy
dry up my sorrows for goodness sake.
My King,
let me worship, I'm down on my knees
Show me Your great favor
I give You everything
my problems, my joy, my heartache
my love… just to be Yours
completely Yours
is all I dream of

day and night…

with the stars above,

giving You my whole heart

because it's all I have to give.

Very Few Can Pay

Saving it
the excess
the scraps
the leftovers
nothing to be lost
there might not be enough
for the future
when we might be in need
of that very thing
you are throwing away
to be carted
to be transformed
from useful to worthless
another mass in a landfill
another shopping trip to fill
the void left in its absence.
When will it ever be enough
to tip the scale
within our minds

within our desire

to have it all

only the best

until satisfaction comes...

at such a high cost

that very few can pay

yet most are willing

to run the unwinnable race

until the end

then lie on a deathbed

full of regret

wishing they had only lived

the life they'd been given

and become wise enough to know

having more money

having more things

does not always equate

to having 'the abundant life'.

At the Water's Edge

Today is a day that will stand out
amongst the rest
my mind is changed
a new course has been laid
I'm free... free at last.
Every single circumstance
that tied me to the past
has been cut loose
no longer am I bound
to result-less reasoning...
my life is being renewed.

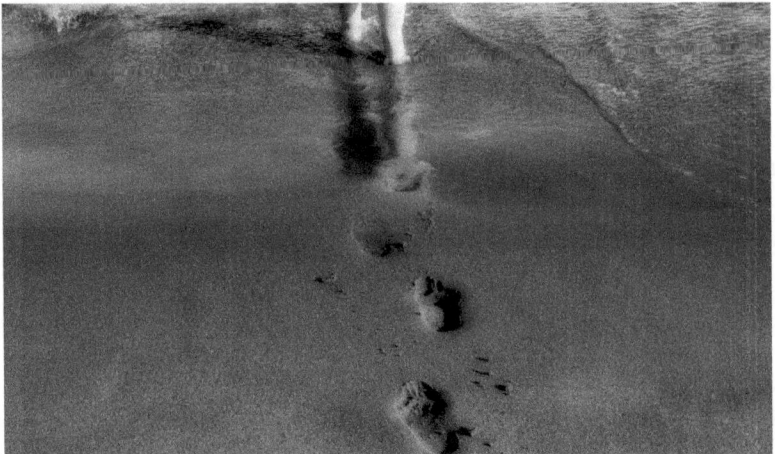

You met me at the water's edge as my feet entered in…

within that very moment it became completely apparent

I would never be the same again.

Without verbal notice, I fell back into the water

shedding the old me… lifting up, I stood…

a new life before me, full of honor and grace.

All because of the One

with the most precious name

Jesus, Jesus… Jesus.

Speak to the Heart

I don't want to stop.
Don't make me stop.
Don't take away the one thing
I truly love to do.
As the years roll on,
lines etched across my face,
my hand grows weak;
still the pen is placed between the fingers
commanded by a brain to write the words
that will be read by someone; by anyone
who knows my heart
who feels my worth,
whether in my presence or on the page
knowing my only hope in life
is to capture a feeling
that could survive the passage of time;
to speak to the heart
of the person reading these lines
and give them a gift very rare to find

in a world of madness…

with so many souls- unkind,

but today – beloved,

maybe your eyes will be open to the truth.

Our Plan

Instant satisfaction when you walk through the door

saying hello, not shying away

it was easy to tell you have been looking for me

or someone like me for a very long time,

the answer to your dreams

came from the relief

as the tension released in your voice

your eyes followed every move of my face

searching for confirmation

words could never say…

that I was your lady; you were my man

together we would build our new world.

No one except we two would make our plan

to marry, to live

become each other's other half

there was nothing to lose

only much to be had within our union

God would provide…

never ever worry, rarely ever cry,

blessed we would always be

blessed by day - blessed at night.

You walked through the door...

I was silently praying you'd say hello.

He's Chasing After You

He's with me!

He's in me!

Whom shall I fear?

The prince of this world trembles at His name.

Defeated at the cross,

he uses shame… to kill and destroy so many lost souls

whose eyes are shut and whose ears can't hear

the gospel truth…

God is not mad,

He's chasing after you,

only to love… to cherish… to hold you in His arms.

He's seeking to save those who are lost.

Do you feel lost?

Call out His name.

Believe He died for you

and your life will never be the same.

charna ainsworth

JESUS
NAME ABOVE ALL NAME

Heaven is My Home

that heaven doesn't seem too far away...
then I can rest, knowing someday
I'll walk down the streets of gold
holding the hand of my savior, Jesus

as He says welcome home.

Soldiers of Light

Formed in a foreign land
at such a time as this...
He sent soldiers of light
to keep watch and protect
His beloved creation
from ruin in this fallen world.
Invisible within the veil,
taking His commands,
saving my life again and again
without a thank you
without my praise
no acknowledgement, not a single word said.
Does an Angel complain?
Would they dare,
if their assignment is a human that doesn't care?
What about an atheist?
Does their Angel quit, pack it up and go home?
If they are not wanted, what else could be done?
Can you grieve your Angel?...

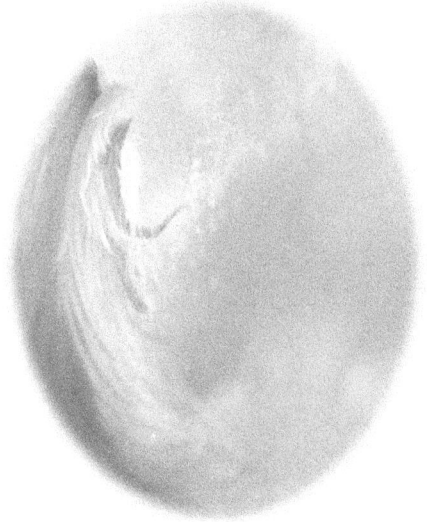

Certainly, most people do…
they look a lot like me,
some look a lot like you.

When I Sing Your Praise

My heart burns with passion
at the very sound of Your name.
Fire fills my soul,
when I'm in Your presence.
All my worries disappear,
when I sing Your praise…
the burdens they leave
when I fall to my knees and pray.
Dead faith comes alive
where two or more are gathered.
Your spoken word
heals dry bones;
in You I'm sanctified…
filled with the Holy Spirit.
Now that I'm in You
I'm never alone.

Birth to Death

Precious child
He knows your name
You're in His every thought
there's nothing on earth
more important than His love.
Don't search
your whole life through
for treasures
you'll never be able to keep...
give your trust to Jesus
He is the one
who will set you free,
from desires in this world
that'll keep you bound in chains.
Search for His blessings
they'll be more than enough
to fulfill your every need
from birth to death.
He is the only way,

my daughter,

in Jesus...

you have an eternal friend.

It Was Me

I've searched for a long time
but always come up short.
Lessons have been learned,
corrections have been made
still, nothing helps
like the sound of Your voice…
leading me down the path
of where You want me to be,
every step fulfilling the promises
Your word points out to me.
Scriptures found
in the nick of time
to save me from myself…
now I find,
as I search the past
You were always here,
always had my back
in all those lonely moments
in the depths of my despair

You were the light in the darkness,

the only one who cared…

if I lived another day

another week

another hour...

and to think

You took the nails

that should have been for me

cause I would have been the one shouting

kill Jesus, set the murderer free.

Now I can so clearly see

that the murderer You saved

all along... it was me.

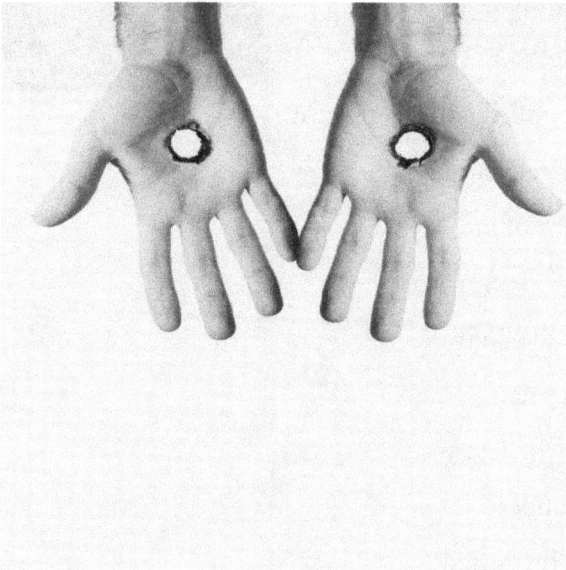

Filled With Your Spirit

Nothing about this is comfortable
it's beyond awkward for me
to walk into a church
where no one recognizes me,
extend my hand
tell a stranger hello
knowing that this person
cannot see my soul
and how my heart
burns for You;
How I'm filled with Your spirit.
All the stranger sees
is the part of me
that truly doesn't matter
because the body
is not eternal…
soon it will pass away
but I wonder
how I'd be treated

charna ainsworth

if they could see

the real me today.

In a Watery Grave

Falling back
water covers the old me,
buried forever
in a watery grave
are all the things
about me
that I couldn't take
into my new life.
Coming up
dripping wet
the life ahead
with no regrets,
no condemnation falls upon me
my eyes are open,
now I see
clearly…
more clearly than ever before
You whispered my name
I walked through *the door*,

found love was waiting

to set me free

baptized in fire-filled water

burned a passion for You in me.

Listen Instead

Walking down the same road I've walked a thousand times,

searching for a change before we drift apart…

leaving no stone unturned,

I speak Your name.

You send the comforter… again, and again

to lighten the burden

to separate fact from fiction.

Now, as I kick the dirt…

He is always listening to my words.

Too many words coming out of my mouth,

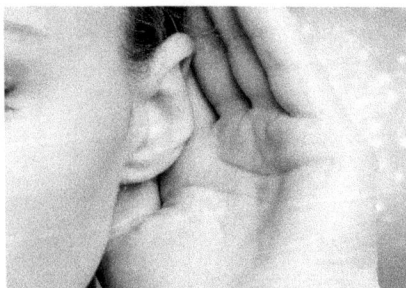

causing division

causing strife

every word tearing me down.

Be quiet -

Don't speak -

Listen instead.

Everyday open your Bible

read the words written in red,

they are health for your body

marrow to your bones.

They will save you from sorrow in this life;

Those same words will bring you home.

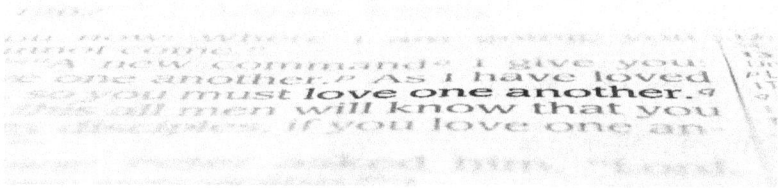

Angel Whispers

Father of peace,

come fill the air…

let Your presence be known.

An atmosphere so rare;

Sinners and saints

fall to their knees

weeping for joy,

all burdens released.

For a moment

the only sound heard

is the whispers of Angels,

speaking Your praise

as another soul

knows they are saved;

Transformed by Your presence,

they walk through The Gate

...so narrow the way,

few ever find

the Prince of Peace.

How blessed are they

who can say...

He's a friend of mine.

I Call Out Your Name

When I'm weak,
when I'm weary…
I call out Your name.
Your Holy Spirit comforts me.
I'm no longer afraid
of what may happen.
The words of accusation
twisting in my mind,
what she might have said…
the things he might think;
Invisible warfare
draining the life out of me.
So, I call out Your name,
knowing You protect me
from everything in this world
my eyes can't see.

A New Name

In my life before You

I did what I wanted to do.

Lies rolled off my tongue,

never cared if I hurt anyone…

laughed at fear,

spit remorse in its face,

straddled the fence

every step along the way.

Called out Your name when I got hurt,

forgot who You were at the end of the day

as darkness took over the night

hiding dirty deeds…

of things left unsaid,

You saw me at my very worst

completely broken

utterly abandoned

by every person

who'd already taken whatever they wanted

from the poor; the needy.

I became so desperate…

for change.

You were waiting,

sweetly calling my name

lifted me up out of the mire

out of the pit…

gave me a new name;

A reason to live.

Crushed the chains

that weighed me down,

filled me with Your Spirit

till I was facedown

worshipping Your goodness…

for a soul such as I;

I never deserved it

but Your Grace lifted me high.

No longer do I wonder what this life is about.

I hold tight to Your promises

knowing only good will come out

of every situation I'm in.

You came…

shed Your blood

for me to have an abundant life.

The world can look at me

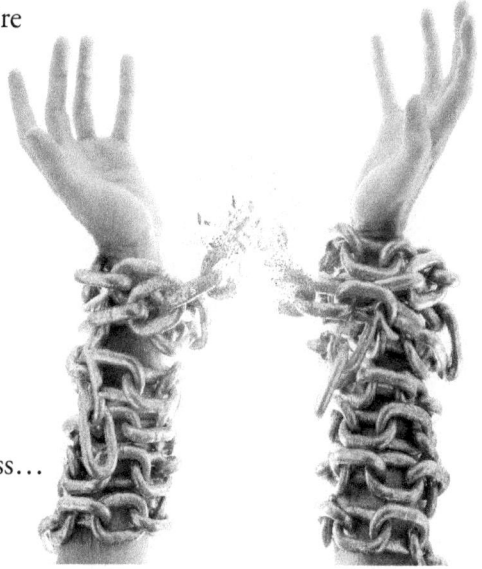

and plainly see

I rest in the palm of Your hand…

blessed with eternal life.

The Prayer In My Heart

Holy Spirit be with me
save my soul
from the one
who despitefully uses me,
who vexes my spirit.
Give me peace
as only You can do.
Hold on to me gently,
help me keep my eyes on You,
learning Your ways
to become more like You
-no matter what I face-
is the prayer in my heart.
No one can hear me say it…
but if actions speak-
I say it again and again,
to the beggar
to the thief
even to friends who abandoned me

because… *I adore You.*

Looking into the eyes of Love…

every kindness I couldn't pay

is now so easy to do.

Everything Is Okay

If I should stumble,

if I should fall,

if my foot should slip

from the narrow path...

would You be there to judge

to condemn

to help me up...

bringing my feet

to stable ground,

holding my hand,

leading me forward...

with a guiding voice

whispering... everything is okay?

Worshipping You

Someday soon I'll see Your face
smiling back at me.
Well done, good and faithful servant...
These words You'll say to me
because I loved the unlovable
I've forgiven the unforgivable
only Your grace set me free
from seeking vengeance
against my enemies,
the ones who sought vengeance
against me.
I've given to the poor
both in spirit
and in love,
poured out my heart in song
worshipping You.
The strong and mighty one
who will look at my life
and say...

you had to be forgiven

much more than most,

just look how much you loved

the least of these I placed

in the paths of your life

even when you thought

I wasn't there

Through you I taught them

through you I fed them -

My precious sheep…

no longer counted among the lost.

After The Last Call

Without trust

       without truth

what can my heart feel?

Afraid to hope…

lest to dream

of everything

turning out okay.

It's a runaway train -

tickets all sold…

no way to get out;

strapped in for life,

till your last breath…

no, you can't hold it,

this ride is not about to end.

So many faces are coming

you'll never remember them all,

none of them are staying

after the last call.

On and on your journey will go,

at times you will feel alone

then looking back

My loving arms around you

will let you know you're finally home.

One Song

What I was taught
while growing up
the words that ruled
my every thought was
sex, drugs, and rock'n'roll.
Those words were the dream
they spoke of destiny
setting me on a path
to places I'd never seen.
Deep in the valley
of needing more
and more and more
I heard a song
on the radio.
Hands and feet...
I want to be Your hands and feet;
Didn't know exactly
what that would mean
but my heart longed for it.

The church doors opened
I sat in the pew
learning new words to live by
the words to eternal life.

Opened Eyes

Not everyone has faith
in Jesus Christ
only those who believe in the power of His name.
Those are the ones
who find the way so very few find
in this world of so much make-believe.

It's hard to tell the truth from a lie.
You need opened ears and opened eyes
to find the proof
that love still exists.

No matter which scholar argues you down
determined to sway
your impressionable heart to believe
there is no God,
there never was…
leaving a confused mind
to choose.

He Is Near

Have faith in God
not in mankind
believe in the promises
written in a book
by divine inspiration
not the words spoken
by God's creation,
that fall and fail...
who lie and cheat,
never ever fulfilling the lives
that were meant to be...
full and everlasting
each day spent in God's light,
now, only a shadow,
a moment of His presence
      remains...
but oh, those moments
to feel He is near
grows my faith

beyond measure.
It will grow yours
if you dare
to believe.

A Strangers Prayer

Open my eyes so I may see what's happening in the spirit realm.
I know I would fight harder if given spiritual sight…
my prayers would not cease because then I would see
what's truly troubling me;
And them… the ones I pray for
never knowing their names
people I pass on the street or during a walk in the park,
the ones sitting near at a baseball game
who will never know me
never know my name
but I said a prayer for them just the same
even though I can't see the true nature of their enemy
or how deep their worry goes.
The Holy Spirit guides these blind eyes
to pray for a stranger,
even those who don't believe
in hopes a simple prayer
might change their fate in eternity.

Left Behind

Where would I be without Your love…
certainly not here,
not safe… not sound
my life would look like everyone else
… in the world
not like the chosen, not like the few

who hear the call.. who answer it
to only find in order to serve
everything once important must be left behind
because holiness required to see God
is hidden for the ones who seek… never giving up

until they find the deep meaning of the story
about God's only son.

Calling Forth My Destiny

There's nowhere I can go
Your eyes can't see me…
no depth too deep
no mountain too high
Your love won't find me.
Though the road seems long
        the task hard…
You make me strong,
even at my weakest.
There's nowhere I want to go
if You are not with me.
I'm afraid of what lurks
        beyond the veil
my eyes can't see,
though I know nothing can separate me.
I search and I seek
to continuously be overshadowed
by Your love
that's calling forth my destiny

despite this world

and its many mysteries

my soul longs for the gifts

only the Holy Spirit can give to me.

Dirty Nails

It's a funny feeling
to feel so un-alone…
like every 'being' in the universe
is happy to cheer you on.
The pats on the back,
saying I knew you could do it.
Confidence soars
to heights never known before
as success sinks in
covering the years of struggle
cleansing the dirty nails
that dug in
staying the course
when others would have let go
when others would have failed
we just keep toiling away
knowing the hard work
would pay someday.
Now our someday is here

amid the cheers.

I will only allow myself

      one tear;

and it for joy.

Mountains Without Names

Hours spent searching…
yes… seeking Your face.
A word or two
to know I'm in Your grace
        …Your will
not led astray.
Not going my own way;
Climbing mountains without names,
following paths that lead to nowhere
except to the moment…
I fall to my knees,
asking, "Jesus, where are You?"
Tell me Your will for my life.
The search will be over.
Still, I'll seek You
all of my days…
finding You in the light of her eyes;
When there's a rainbow in the sky,
and when I see Your fingerprints on my life.

The Only Choice

Show me Your mercy, God.

I didn't want to fail.

It's always one step forward

two steps back.

The feeling of going nowhere…

weighs heavy on this heart

that was so full of love.

Never saw this coming…

me, with a downcast spirit

unable to see truth

not anywhere I go

not in anything they do

makes my soul retreat;

living a life behind the scenes

of cold stares and social media bullies.

How did life change …so suddenly?

It's hard to recognize my place in all this tragedy.

Was I really meant to hide?

The storms keep coming…

I pray You give me a voice.

There's not a doubt

in this world…

choosing to love is the only choice.

Rich

Pardon me, Sir

might you have the time?

Jesus is calling

His voice whispers through mine,

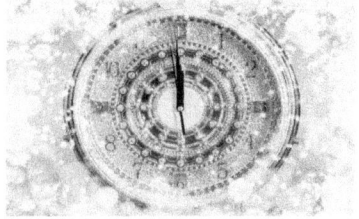

as I speak of His goodness

what He's done for me.

You see, there's only one reason I'm still alive...

The Prince of Peace.

My testimony is rich

because of my Savior's love,

His blood covers my many sins

committed mostly in youth

before I knew anything

except hate, lies, and drugs.

You see, I was the lost...

now I'm the found.

My eyes are opened

to truth and light,

I no longer fear mankind...

what they can do or say

because I have a friend in Jesus

and no one can take that away.

He is Holy

Praise the one who calls you by name.

The one who created the oceans.

He spoke the stars into the sky.

Thought up every living creature

you can and cannot see.

He is holy!

So worthy to be praised…

He lifts the hopeless

out of a self-dug grave,

in His peace

they find amazing grace.

His eyes are searching

for the lost

to be found

when the name Jesus is spoken

no earthly chains can keep them bound.

Glory to the one who never sleeps!

His ears hear your prayers.

He knows when you weep.

Nothing will He withhold

from the ones who praise His name.

All of heaven awaits… those who worship

the everlasting King of Kings.

charna ainsworth

Most Precious Name

In the presence of Your love
is where I want to be,
feeling You here
as I kneel to the floor to worship and praise
the one who gave me
the most precious name...
daughter, son, friend,
set apart; never alone again.
I seek You.
I find You.
The throne of God feels like home
when I'm kneeling at Your feet
praising Your kindness...
all You've done for me.
Your presence surrounds me;
it makes me whole.
I surrender it all...
every hardship I've known.
They are nothing compared

charna ainsworth

to the love that I feel

when casting my cares upon You.

Precious Truth

One day you will learn
one day you will find
I've always been with you
even during the toughest times.
My mercy has held back
the wall of fear
threatening to fall upon you,
crushing your spirit beyond repair.
I watch and I wonder
why do you feel so alone?
I promised I'd never leave you.
With Me, you will always be home.
There is no distance...
between your heart and mine,
no measure of sin
no mountain to high
to separate you from your destiny
of being one...
you belong in the Trinity
Father, Spirit, and Son.

Crying Out

There were days of blindness...
seeking only pleasure,
never thinking about pain
when I did what I wanted,
didn't care what happened
only living for the moment
just wanting to have fun,
took too many chances
life could have taken a bad turn
often, I ran from trouble
taking a nosedive when I turned,
the days were uncounted
for anything good or sane...
running down a one-way street
until I cried out Your name.
Now, nothing is the same
because I seek Your grace,
selfishness has ceased
having its hold on me.

Your words are written

on the tablet of my heart.

I seek Your glory…

from Your love I will never depart.

A Beautiful Testimony

Butterflies are calling
the sound of their wings
carried on the wind
whisper the words
they're unable to say.
It's not a secret,
all are wise to their destiny...
float
      flutter
            fly
such beauty fills the mind,
watching the colors
the Lord intertwined
in each wing
a beautiful testimony
of His delight
to bless His creation and proclaim His glory
in the simplicity and diversity
of a butterfly's wings.

Adoption Day

When the world brings me to my knees
it is Your hand that holds and protects me,
so… I am of good courage
because the Lord strengthens me.
You see, my hope is in Him
and He is all that I will ever need.
I am blessed
for I am forgiven
all my transgressions are gone.
I am the beloved.
I am the redeemed.
I am a chosen one,
and with my adoption
I join the family of my King.
Now I know
when I cried out
the Lord, my God, heard me.

Deep In My Soul

There You are in his eyes.
Oh, how they sparkle and shine
like a clear blue ocean
with rays of sunshine bouncing
upon gentle waves.
I can see You when I look into his eyes.
Then I hear You in the sound of his voice
blending so perfectly with inspired music
the lyrics strike a chord deep in my soul
that only You know…
yet it's still his voice.
His feet turned toward me
bringing him closer with every step,
only complete surrender
guides him directly to me…
because of You.
Hands reach out, as a gentleman would do…
helping me to my feet.
With purpose and a destiny,

I search my mind

and remember what I read;

Who will go?

Here I am - send me.

Judgement, Gossip and Hate

I know the question You will ask when this life is over...

Did I learn to love?

As I gaze out across this shining sea called humanity, I ponder my answer.

It's been easy to love my family even when they treated me wrong.

When some of my church members blew me away with judgment, gossip,

and hate

I believed they were the chosen so, I loved them anyway.

When my good friends turned to enemies, I loved them from afar.

Really, now, that I think of it… I've almost loved them all.

There were those who scarred me so deeply, I prayed for their demise…

prayed the same scriptures King David wrote in Psalm 109.

The hate was so real there was no room for love.

So, how will I answer?

What will I say to my Father in heaven on judgment day?

When he asks one simple question...

Did you learn to love?

Yes, God, I did. See... even my scars reveal the depths of my decision to love.

charna ainsworth

Life Or Death

Trapped in words rolling off the tongue

meant to love

should have

could have

spoken blessings

instead of curses.

Ignorant to the fact

a child would pay dearly

for that moment…

into adulthood and beyond.

Never escaping

the proficiency of words

-negative

-poisoning

every dream

the child ever dreamed

until…

she heard

a blessing spoke over her

and she opened

to receive

the words

which erased

the curses,

carried like burdens

for a generation.

The blessing

opened her eyes

to see,

opened her ears

to hear,

opened her heart

to dream again…

knowing this time

doors would be open

that no man could shut.

The curses

on her life

fell away…

revealing the depth

of God's blessings,

saved up for this day.

They Don't Hear Me

When the curse lifted, I could feel joy again.
My hunger,
no longer driven by food…
became a deep desire to be closer to Him,
to feel His glory
to be in His presence
to know His name
because of thankfulness
a miracle performed
a sign I'm not alone
… the answer to prayer.
Everyone looks at me
like I'm the same.
I mention the blessing
I received;
they don't hear me
but I'm screaming
out loud.
Look at me!

I'm changed.

I had a Holy Ghost experience…

I will never be the same.

A man I never met,

spoke a blessing over me…

took away the curse

of always being hungry

which may not sound like much

to the average Joe

but to me

it is a miracle,

and I want the whole world to know

that God is still there.

He's sitting on the throne.

It's by the blood of Jesus Christ

that I'm able to stand

and testify

of beauty for ashes

and the redemption of my life.

Growing Old

I got the news today

that Satan wants me to believe.

Something's wrong with your body,

we need you to come back in…

a few more tests

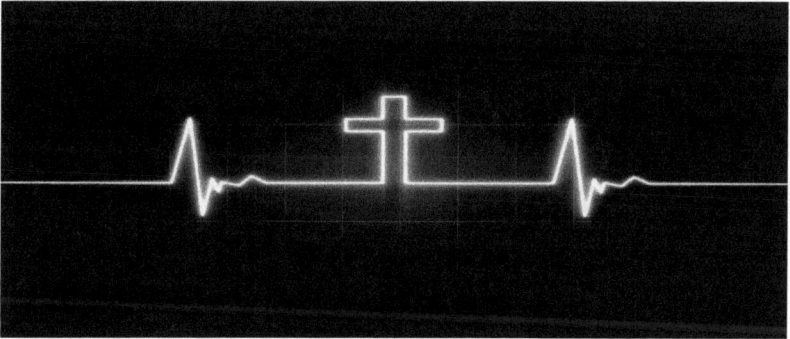

then we'll be able to tell if next year will be happy

or if you'll be going through hell.

There's one thing these people don't understand about being a child of God;

their medical test results mean little to me,

I've got the Holy Spirit in my soul.

He says I'm going to grow old…

fulfill every dream

God put inside of me

and fulfill my destiny.

The Book of Life

Everything I am is enough.
He loves me just the way I am.
There's no need to worry,
my Father knows everything,
He completely accepts me…
my strengths, my weaknesses
my joys and sorrows,
He sees every part of me
the good and the bad.
What a friend we have
in the one who created it all.
Why He loves me so
I'll never really know
because I've let him down
more times than I can count
been so mad at Him;
blamed Him for things
that now I know
were not His fault
cried out why don't You love me

when things didn't go my way.
Still, He stood beside me
patiently guiding my stubborn feet
down a narrow path
lined with rocks and thorns
refusing to let me turn back
even when I begged
sat down in the dirt
cried and cried
He wouldn't let me
return to my old life.
So many days I wondered…
why doesn't He just let me go
I don't deserve His mercy
I don't deserve His love.
Those were the days
Jesus would hold me tight
He would whisper words…
those words led me to life,
the life He spoke of;
The abundant life
where your leaf doesn't wither
where your fruit becomes His delight
and your name
He gets to write
in the book of life.

God's Glorious Light

Diamonds never shined brighter
than when reflecting God's glorious light
nor have I seen
more love reflecting
than when I looked
into my Father's eyes.
His words came flowing
like a river through me.
He is all that I want
or will ever need
and someday soon
this will not be
a dream
a vision
something in my mind.
No, one day I'll be going home
somewhere far from here
up high in the sky.
Up there I will sparkle,

I'll shine like never before

and when I find the one

who lovingly took my place...

I will be home forevermore.

At Your Feet

The clay is in Your hands.
Do as You will…
there's no resistance,
easily I bend
and stretch
at the touch of Your fingertips
releasing my burdens and cares
of what I should be
there at Your feet
where rivers of life flow
crystal clear as new glass.
The Potter is my friend,
He knows my needs
I never have to ask.
Still, I do
because I want to talk to Him
on good days and bad.
I want nothing more
than to yield to The Potter
… to be clay in His hands.

If I Could Be Perfect

Oh, how you're wrapped up

in things the world wants you to see

blinding your eternal soul

with things that are not eternal.

The striving

the worry,

anxiety ruling your thoughts…

always thinking if you were perfect

you could have it all,

be famous and rich

flying around the world in your private jet

going from party to party

snapping up selfies to share with your followers

a lifestyle they're not good enough

… to get;

but if they could see you when you're all alone…

broken and crying out to a God you've never known

asking why…

why do I have so much

but still feel so empty inside;

they would know

the life you post

shows nothing but a lie.

Beneath The Surface

Safe and secure

within the arms of the only true love

I've ever known.

Sheltered from life's storms,

never abandoned

never alone

watched over like a precious stone.

Too valuable;

not fully understanding

my worth to You.

My role in this world,

like ink... so quick to dry,

a blink of the eye...

sweet time does pass

and the meaning of purpose,

the reason for birth

lingers beneath my surface

like waves ready to crash

the shores of life

moving grains of sand

reshaping my path

moment by moment

until the task is complete.

Words have Power

My Tiny Voice

Poured out upon the stage

judgment in their eyes

judgment from their lips.

Whoa! What they think of me.

Never free from the gossip

swimming in their heads.

No wonder I'm silent

considering the weapons, they bare.

Like a two-edged sword

tongues move up and down

destroying many lives
yet I stand on solid ground.

Embraced by truth,
surrounded by chariots of fire
when I speak in tongues
all of heaven hears

my tiny voice

-and the ones who speak unkindly
to entertain themselves
will find out what
'judge not' really means
someday...
not too far away
when He returns for me.

Never Look Back

In a moment grey faded to black.

Fallen... under attack

for my love of the one they call Jesus.

Lines drawn blurring the edge

of what's seeable and what is felt.

Shoving me down...

grasping for His hand,

on knees now uttering words that can't be said.

In my dreams poetry comes

linking lives...

creating syllables is fruitless;

It can't be undone.

There is only a future...

a white wall divides me from the past,

it glows with the light

      of love.

My savior is saying -never look back

but if you do... if you can't resist looking over your shoulder...

in a moment you'll see the darkest black change to white

glowing with light

enough to make visible the path left to walk

nowhere else to go.

Now… I'm bringing you home.

A Thousand Lies

Once upon a time
I thought I knew it all
no one could tell me
what I needed to do.
I was the captain...

sink or sail
even when walking through hell
I did as I pleased.

Smart enough to run the ship

around the world;

Running aground

a time or two...

still, running -

believing there was no end

of good luck...

of the blessing.

Only to finally grow up

to witness

seeds are sown...

though wild

still, they grow.

The harvest,

I avoid with thoughts

of running

to some distant shore

hoping the past cannot follow

the woman I see

in the mirror now

...someone similar

to who I use to be

staring into eyes

that have lived

a thousand lives…

beaten and bruised

by a thousand lies.

The promises broken-

left my spirit damaged

from the tears

of too many days

that no one cared;

Not even I.

Those seeds grew a vine

choking the last days

of a misguided life.

Is there anyone who can

cut them away

so I can breathe?

Will He bring a shovel

to dig up the roots

from around my feet?

My soul is free

and ready to run...

Will He come

and rescue the one

who didn't stay?

Thought the ninety-nine

were lost...

thought they didn't know the way.

The vines that grow

thick and strong

holding me back

from the abundant life

will never die

on their own.

Cut me free...

I'll be free.

Dig up the roots.

Let me run to You.

Cast them in the fire

that was never

meant for me.

Show me Your mercy.

Your grace has set me free.

www.charnaainsworth.com

Reviews are welcomed and appreciated. Links to multiple book venues are located at: www.charnaainsworth.com

Cherished reader,

The reason I write is for *You,* and every other person who is searching for truth. My hope is you will read these words and know you are not alone. With every line, with each poem, I poured out my heart. Thank you so much for reading *I Will Adore You Christian Poetry.* You are appreciated more than you will ever know.

about the poet -

Charna Ainsworth is a novelist and an award-winning poet. She lives in small southern town with her family.

Also Available From Charna Ainsworth

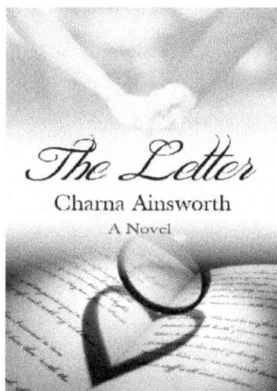

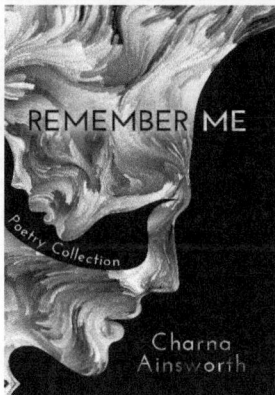

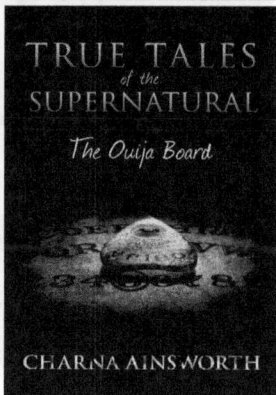

The Letter
Charna Ainsworth
A Novel

Shades of *Persuasion*
Charna Ainsworth
A Novel

MOUNTAIN of GOD
The Journey

CHARNA AINSWORTH

UNLIKELY CHRISTIAN
Poetry Collection
Charna Ainsworth

REMEMBER ME
Poetry Collection
Charna Ainsworth

TRUE TALES of the SUPERNATURAL
The Ouija Board

CHARNA AINSWORTH

More Great Books by Charna Ainsworth

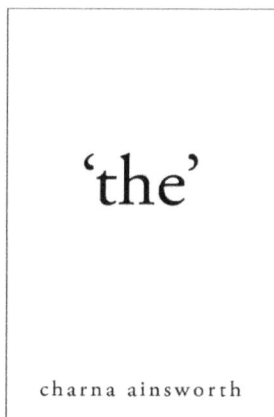

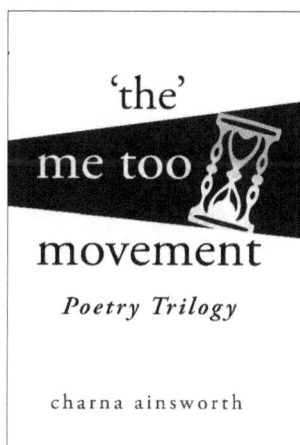

'the'

charna ainsworth

movement

charna ainsworth

me too

their
time
is
up

charna ainsworth

'the'
me too
movement

Poetry Trilogy

charna ainsworth